Joe DiMaggio Moves Like Liquid Light

Joe DiMaggio Moves Like Liquid Light

poems

Loren Broaddus

Andrews McMeel
PUBLISHING®

For Marilyn, Loren Michael, and Catherine, always.

In memory of Marlis Meyer. For Melvin Meyer.

In memory of my grandparents—Robert and Bunny Long, and Dolly and Loren Broaddus—all, in one way or another, were poets.

For my parents, Loren and Nancy, who early on exposed my brothers and me to baseball, and to many other good things.

And in memory of Carrie Turner.

"It's all about the light."

—Jim Mayfield, Ozarks photographer

"I think there are only three things that America will be known for 2,000 years from now . . . jazz music, the Constitution, and baseball."

—*Gerald Early, poet*

Poems

Triumvirate

There is the football scene,
or two, and the Christmas
ice skating, but go deep
into Charlie Brown's longings,
pain, excitement, no matter
rain, snow, sun, or season, there is
baseball, winning or (mostly)
losing, all set to Vince Guaraldi's
jazz trio casting its fate
to the wind. What we need
is a conference on the mound
between Charlie Brown and his
brain trust—Lucy, Linus,
and Schroeder debating
whether Madisonian checks
and balances give special interest
groups too much sway in a democracy,
as Snoopy waits patiently to resume
his position at shortstop,
his fielding as fine
as the deft fingers of Thelonious Monk.

Sacrifice

Bean counters, data men,
ridicule the sacrifice bunt,
labeling it a wasted out, old-
fashioned and small, unsupportable
by crunched numbers, foolish. Yet
it moves the runner, creating
a ballet of motion, artfully
executed, an act wholly beyond
oneself, nearing grace, immeasurable,
immeasurably lost
in an age of artless analytics.

"Houston Astrodome at 50—
The Global 'Wonder' Now a Decaying Shell"

—Reuters headline, April 10, 2015

Fenway Park, built in 1912, sets record
for consecutive sellouts at 820 games
from 2003 to 2013.

Houston, 1965

We look around smugly
at old-fashioned ballparks
and laugh. The *future*
is where we live, not the dusty
past where grass needs sunlight
and water, where games
wash away in rain, or are played
in raging waves of heat. No
one wants to watch baseball
like that. In all confidence,
we are too smart for such
shenanigans. Bulldoze the old,
and in with the Astrodome.
We know many more will
follow, moving with the future,
its breathtaking taming
of nature, its climate control,
its controlling engineered
technology, igniting us
into worlds of our own making.
No one will ever want
the old-fashioned ballpark
again. Grow or go, you
dinosaurs of tradition,
there is no going back.

A Response to the Late Bertrand Russell After Reading his Quote That the Trouble with the World Is That the Stupid Are Cocksure and the Intelligent Are Full of Doubt

Are you certain?

—*March 15, 2012*

"I think a baseball field must be the most beautiful thing in the world. It's so honest and precise."

—Jim Lefebvre, quoted in "Love of the Game" by Lowell Cohn,
The Fireside Book of Baseball, *Volume IV*

Winter Road to Clever, Missouri

In this case, Clever
is a place, not
a condition, as we
wind through oak-gray
hills and khaki fields
at rest after simmering
summer work, Highway
14 speckled slightly
from angled, filtered,
pale winter light striking
the pavement. To our left,
as Clever nears, sits
the high school baseball
field, neat and trimmed
and also dormant,
beautiful in its stillness,
far, far away
from tech-driven,
self-referential, cleverness.

Wintering

It's the wintering
trees I have an eye
for, their naked
beauty enveloped
by pale-skinned
January—bare,
honest, three-
dimensional, hiding
nothing, nothing more
to lose, opening
the horizon to Orion's
rising, widening the
lightening sky as
earth rolls over
each morning into
sunlight, beautiful
and subtle as a jazz
trio, Bill Evan's
to be exact, playing
the minimalist,
exquisite *Moonbeams,*
my spirit stripped
of the trivial with
each passing, delicate,
wintering note.

Vanilla

Fields the shade of French vanilla
stretch toward hills of dark oak
lacework, stark against white
sullen sky. Circling, circling
above the somber, silent earth,
a red-tailed hawk floats on the chill,
oblivious to thoughts of warmth,
of fire, of fear. I soak in the peace,
but soon remember fields of green
and long for my bright-eyed wife
and Irish-headed boy.

—*February 2002*

Racing Westward

Long before the jagged, capped mountains
emerged purple from the western
horizon, a small Kansas town presented
itself some distance off to the right, grain
elevator, church spire, water tower all rising
above summer trees bunched under each,
and in the forefront, as we raced westward,
a tree-lined manicured high school baseball
field—bread, water, spirit, soul.

Yogi-metrics

The over-dog is the underdog
since nobody chooses to take
the fork in the road out of the nightclub's
sparse crowd because of its popularity.
Why else would anyone wait
for anything to be over, obviously
only thin ladies singing, to the music
of a jazz trio, the bass player
wondering where everyone is,
stealing a glance at his watch,
noticing it's getting late
awfully early out there.

Ballpark Tavern

The Ballpark Tavern stands
at the corner of West and Madison,
near no ballpark, seemingly
misnamed, surrounded by white
chat parking lot, neatly mown
grass, and modest, small houses
lining all four directions of tree-lined
neighborhood street. From outside,
nothing but the name hints that
on this spot played the hated Chicago
Cubs' AAA farm team for only one
full summer, the first summer of war
in Korea, in this Cardinal-red town.
Now, ghosts of forgotten
outfielders, their dreams in front
of them then, call for fly balls
in the rich summer twilight,
as patrons hear only crunched
gravel underfoot as they make their way
to their cars after a couple
of friendly after-work cold ones
at the Ballpark, yet another
day slipping into echoes.

Meeting Mike Sweeney

When I met him, we both
remembered the ninth inning
shoulder-high fastball he drilled
into the gap in right center
for a walk-off Father's Day
double against the Giants in 2003,
the game a gift from my wife,
the crowd so loud I could not hear
our two-year-old son's startled
crying from the roar, though quickly
I lifted him to my chest, smiling, as
we all felt lifted by Sweeney's
hit—a hit ten years later I thought
he would have surely forgotten
after sixteen Big League seasons,
yet when I told him of my memory,
we eagerly finished each other's
sentences with details, like two
grown men unexpectedly
realizing at a business meeting
that they share the same
childhoods from the same
neighborhood, know the same
faces, the same summer games,

from a time now long
gone, or maybe glimpsed
outside of time when all
moments are lifted moments,
like meeting Mike Sweeney.

Whales

Are we not all, down deep,
Captain Ahabs? Maybe not
in vengeance but in envy
of the whale, mammals
like us, yet navigating
sun-shafted, blue-hued
depths for hours, loosed
from binding gravity
and friction only to burst
through the salty ceiling
into bright light, airborne,
to breathe deeply.

"Once, Cool Papa Bell hit a line drive right past my ear. I turned around and the ball hit his ass sliding into second."

—*Satchel Paige*

James Thomas "Cool Papa" Bell

Legacies

Black as soothing nightfall,
after glaring summer sunlight, Carrie
cared for the blonde granddaughter
of Mister William, delighting in her,
daily telling the child stories
of Joe DiMaggio, the way he rounded
second base like liquid light, and
later of Mickey Mantle flying too close
to the sun, but what speed, what
power in the wrists, always omitting
from the tale the Jim Crow section
of the stands from which she was forced
to watch. She helped the little girl
grow, gain footing in a swirling world,
maybe hoping the great-grandson
someday far off will take to baseball,
and to baseball games take his children,
children who might hear histories
told of Bud Fowler and Moses Fleetwood
Walker, Satchel Paige, Cool Papa Bell,
and Jack Roosevelt Robinson, even later still
attempting to understand that simple answers
cannot begin to explain complicated legacies.

Cool Papa Bell at Bedtime

Catherine always asked
for bedtime stories
about princesses playing
baseball with Cool Papa Bell,
the only seven-year-old girl
I knew requesting tales
of romance mixed with quicksilver
speed, listening intently
as Cool Papa scores
from second on a bunt,
and beats out two-hop
ground balls to short,
playing on the same
team as this evening's royal
heroine, even famously
out-running electricity,
and almost, *almost* keeping
up with the princess,
as Catherine eases
smiling into sleep.

Vinegar and Wine

We think we understand Cobb,
the fierce angry energy roiling
from every pore, the refusal
to lose, the intimidating
high spikes, the bitter chipped
calculated abandon.

Mathewson is the mystery,
a gentle soul mowing down
batters like fields of alfalfa,
each man elite, drawing strength
and power from two distinct
deep wells, water from one tasting
of vinegar, the other of wine.

F1

Just a reminder
that nature exists still,
no matter the thickness
of our walls.

Just a reminder
our piece of the puzzle
is smaller than people
like to think.

Liberty Park, 1924

In Memory of Dolly McPherson Broaddus

She was seventeen,
working late
at the department store
on Ohio street,
walking alone home
from the end
of the trolley line
across a darkened
Liberty Park when
all lit up like sunburst
in the winter bleakness
as hooded figures
stood defiantly silhouetted
circling around a flaming
glowing cross where
second base should
have been on the nearby
ball diamond, rally-starting
lined doubles into the gap
in happier, warmer times
long forgotten on this night,
the terror still in her
eyes sixty years later
as the story unwinds
like a fastball under her chin.

Texas League Foul Ball

As I remember it,
the right-handed hitter
pulled a pitch hard
foul on one hop, hitting
the rolled-up tarp,
careening airborne
into the stands, all
as the stranger stood,
five rows up, catching
the ball bare-handed,
lefty, over his head,
just like that, sitting
quickly, quietly slipping
his prize to a nearby
child, given in grace,
received in childlike
prideless joy.

"A ballgame is a wonderful place to visit with someone you love."

—*George W. Bush*

Purple

For Marilyn

Cold flowed in
like last winter's
last laugh on that
early June evening
at Old Busch—Royals
visiting Cardinals,
a weekend away
we knew might change
our life together,
spark profundity,
become part of our
story. Walking
across a crosswalk
toward the stadium
with thousands
of red-wearing
St. Louisans, a
child holding his
father's hand, peering
over his shoulder
at us holding each
other's hands, you
in your bright red
McGwire jersey, me

in my blue Sweeney,
says, "Look Daddy, a
mixed-up couple!" Hours
later, long after
the game, we merge
into purple, but not
from the cold.

Thomas Hobbes

For Marilyn

Some days it seems
my former history
professor was correct
in quoting Hobbes, that
existence is ugly, short,
nasty, and brutish—a baseline
of mucus, blood, feces, urine.

There are days, at best,
when the extra-virgin
olive oil on the chicken breasts,
a surprise dinner for you,
burns onto the baking sheet
and stinks up the kitchen, and
outside, it is so cold
our fingertips crack, while
images on the screen show
violence, war, scandal, hatred.

But on other days, our child
reaches up, for the first time,
to hold my hand. The sun speaks
out louder and longer into the late
winter dusk. And some nights
during sweet, exquisite,
delightful moments with
you—a glimpsed timelessness—you
then we, clench eyes tight
as if in pain . . . but we aren't.

—January 28, 2010

Rain-Out

What else that has not
been said is there to say
about rain, as we drive
home on wet slickened
streets from a washed-
out minor league game
at Hammons Field. We
suffer with too little
of the stuff, or too much,
a condition I feel deep
in my bones, and yet slowly
I become conscious
of our five-year-old
daughter singing quietly,
tenderly . . . "I love the rain"
for the next twenty minutes
from her backseat booster seat,
in the sweetest voice.

Solstice Walk

I watched our son calmly
leaning over the padded
crossbar of his stroller, arms
extended out front, fingers
dangling over sea-gray
sidewalk, chin resting on the bar,
honeyed evening light
firing his Irish hair.
Not thinking of shorter days,
nor of teaching in the fall, nor
of coming hectic schedules, nor
fretting the slipperiness
of time, he instead engaged
serenely the delicious
waning light of the longest
day of the year.

—June 2003

My Team Is in the World Series For the First Time in Twenty-Nine Years . . .

And my chest hurts. No lazy
summer listening anymore
on the front porch swing
with simple slow rhythms
of tradition for comfort, my
childhood teams of the '70s and '80s
slick, fast, heart-stopping,
winning back then
with nothing in between but
loyalty and low expectations. Now
again, every pitch roars with
potential, in either direction;
every out like post-Depression
banking, secure; every run
given or gained, explosive;
every moment hinged to the next.
Everywhere disease, death,
loss, war, and suffering rule—I know
this. Game Six means
nothing . . . and yet, my chest hurts.

"My God, Ruth played there and Gehrig. They were heroes and they hit in the same box, ran the same bases. They left their spirits there. I know it."

—Jim Lefebvre, on the first time he played at Yankee Stadium, quoted in "Love of the Game" by Lowell Cohn, The Fireside Book of Baseball, *Volume IV*

Eyes

Their eyes arrest you
from the black and white
photographs—faces of Murderers'
Row, the 1927 New York Yankees.
An amateur, Charles Conlon,
captured these images,
faces only, individual extreme
close-ups, eyes in clear focus, the curve
to the ear becoming less clear.
Ruth is there, the icon; and Gehrig,
the tragic knight. The freckled
centerfielder, Earle Combs,
a religious Kentuckian in a rough
world and tumble sport, peers
through, a somehow accepted,
respected rebel. A pair of eyes
stare from each photograph,
each man then young, famous,
successful, vibrant in a vibrant
age; each man now mysterious,
as the dead always are
to the still-living—echoes of
Dukes Ellington's jazz still
almost audible, an aroma

of admiring young women's
sweet perfume still lingering,
long after they've left the room.

"Why not? His skin is prettier than mine!"

—Catherine Broaddus, age 6, after reading that Jackie Robinson, as a boy, was not allowed to swim in a pool because of his skin color

Jackie Robinson

Jack, 1947

His greatest contribution
maybe is not his remarkable
self-control; or his splendid
athleticism—his speed,
daring, fierceness; or even
his fearful courage. Maybe
it is the way he inspires us
even today to cheer for him,
briefly forgetting bitter histories.

Daughter

She dances at bedtime
in utero. My wife
giggles with each
move. Three months
from meeting this little
one, I already feel
different.

—April 21, 2008

Lost Grace

All along the maple-lined
streets, front porches cradled
chain-hung swings deep
within the half-light
shadow. Shirt sleeved
men, cottoned women
congregated, fanning,
fleeing household heat
onto these half-in,
half-out havens. Neighbor
knew neighbor, spoke
of ovened air, of pennant
chances, of offspring, across
gulfs of fireflied bluegrass.
Knit tight.

Somewhere
within the perfection apparent,
Monarchs, after joyfully
playing the national pastime,
stand heads bowed, gray flannel
uniforms sweat soaked,
in back of Red's Diner, paying

to eat cold sandwiches on a dark
dusty bus, saying grace
lost into night winds.

Have You Noticed . . .

That life here resembles a pitcher
possessing a live fastball
with late movement;
a drop-off-the-tabletop curve;
and a solid setup change-of-pace;
who can get comfortable, settle in,
find the groove, only long enough
to break your heart?

No One Wants to Read
A Poem About a Dog . . .

Too sentimental—the loyal
wet eyes, the frantic
figure-eight making
tail, the eager clicks
in the front hallway
as you arrive home,
his name probably
Jack, all ending in
lifelessness, a sunny
June day under
a favorite tree, which
is why I will never
read a poem about a dog,
let alone write one.

Bill Virdon's Ground Ball

It was hard hit, right
at Tony Kubek, yet
routine as routine
could be, an eighth
inning double play
ground ball, Game
Seven at stake
of the 1960 World Series.
Virdon's scorcher
crazy-hopped into Kubek's
throat, the opening
to a Mazeroski ninth inning
coup d'état,
though also to a decade
of unexpected bounces,
the sixties ripped
by assassinations, war,
riots—an entire culture
countered, the disestablishment
of anything resembling routine.

"Courage is a virtue that President Kennedy most admired. He sought out those people who had demonstrated in some way, whether it was on a battlefield or a baseball diamond . . . that they could be counted on."

—Robert F. Kennedy, 1964 Forward to the memorial edition of Profiles in Courage

Two Lonely Yankees

—October 16, 1962, 3:33pm, Pacific Coast Time

There must be a lonelier place than this,
Ralph Terry must have thought as he stood
on the mound in the bottom
of the ninth inning
of the seventh game
of the World Series, up 1-0, two on, two out.
Matty Alou, the tying run,
walked slowly just outside the line
off third, as Willie Mays led off second,
the winning run, his head turning
side to side to avoid a potential final-out
pick-off play. Staring back at Terry
from the batter's box stood
massive Willie McCovey who
had just blasted a fastball
into the right field seats, but
ten feet foul. All eyes fixed
on Terry, anticipating his next
pitch, guessing his grip on the ball,
the moment hanging thick,
waiting breathless for McCovey
to launch another missile . . .

There must be a lonelier place than this,
John Kennedy must have thought,
at that exact moment,
three thousand miles across a continent,
staring down a map of Soviet
missile sites in Cuba
—Khrushchev's subterfuge—
needing to deliver the perfect pitch
that would not be launched.

Stolen Satisfaction

Lord knows I am
not smart enough
or hard-working
enough to be
a farmer—but
there is some
stolen satisfaction
from the farm
after the lawn
is mowed, trimmed,
and plants watered
that must be a tiny
fraction of the feeling
when the harvest
is in and all is
secured as possible,
for winter.

"I honestly feel it would be best for the country
to keep baseball going."

*—Franklin D. Roosevelt, letter to Kennesaw Mountain Landis,
January 15, 1942*

"They booed Ted Williams too, remember?"

—Lyndon B. Johnson

Splinter

As light spilt across the last day
of the 1941 baseball season,
Ted Williams, the Splendid Splinter,
was hitting .39955 with a double-header
against the Athletics looming. All wondered
if he would take the day off, take a mathematical
round up to magical .400. Bud and Walt, brothers
from Boston, trekked to Shibe Park to find out.
Joe DiMaggio had hit in 56 straight games earlier
this same summer. Would Williams match
his rival's feat with a .400 season? Bud
thought Williams too brave or crazy to watch
from the bench, Walt not so sure. Against the wishes
of his manager, Teddy Ballgame played anyway,
both games, going six for eight, ending at .406,
leaving no doubts, or decades of debates,
the brothers certain history had been witnessed.
Soon after, Walt said goodbye to his brother,
shipping out to Hawaii the next day,
to the battleship Arizona, soon to be splintered.

Blue Monday

We never worked harder
than in Mr. Lollar's sophomore
English class, learning
the intricacies of the five
paragraph essay, listening
in awe as Frost's *Birches*
made us feel something
other than boredom
or confusion, and seeing
for the first time Jim
Morrison and the Doors
on a poster on the inside
of our teacher's closet door. Two
surprises stick in the memory—
a quiet boy's essay earning
an almost impossible to earn
A-, and that overcast
October Monday afternoon
when Mr. Lollar wheeled
in a TV to watch
the Expos play the Dodgers
in the National League
playoffs, the deciding
tension-ridden Game Five,
the older brother of one
of our classmates pitching

the ninth inning for the Expos,
their hard-working ace, giving
up a game-losing home run
to Rick Monday, awkward
silence falling at Stade
Olympique and also in
our own classroom, no one
knowing what to say
to the little brother, a
day Montreal fans know
to this day as Blue Monday.

"Do not imagine that if you meet a really humble man he will be what most people call humble . . . He will not be thinking about humility; he will not be thinking about himself at all."

—Clive Staples Lewis

The Life of Alex Rodriquez

We do
not care to admit it,
but we share the life
of Alex Rodriquez
—the hated Yankee—
his golden, hope-filled
youth; the remarkable
potential; the inability
to cope with expectations,
leading to shortcuts
and rationalizations,
self-centered control,
pride, and a numbing
hollowness within.
Then there is the separation
from the Game, the shame
of truth slicing it all open,
a deeply felt pain as feeling
returns, like tiny needles,
hopefully reaching redemption
in forty-year-old humility,
knowing one's place,
surrendering to a peace
we never knew we needed, yet
we do.

June 6, 2004

Sixty years ago tonight, young
paratroopers, her father among
them, dropped through darkness
into swamps, snagged onto church
steeples, scattered, helpless,
dangling souls soon to lose
all amid fire and firing, their
short stanzas jaggedly ending.

Years later, as the daughter
surveys her English class
of street-smart seventh graders,
the same fate seems
written across their lost grins,
much as she attempts to help
rewrite their poetry.

The Loudest Whisper

In Memory of Jerry Lumpe

His obituary appeared
in the *New York Times,*
a former Yankee infielder
with a World Series ring
and a to-this-day highly
ranked fielding percentage,
a boy from Warsaw, Missouri
living a Major League life,
winning it all alongside
Mantle and Stengel and Yogi
in '58, hitting .301 for his
home state Athletics in '62,
an All-Star and roommates
with Al Kaline as a Tiger '64,
even one day appearing
in a Peanuts comic strip, his name
uttered by Charlie Brown. All this
many dream of, though never do.
But looking back, as light
illuminates his life, he sees
not hard-hit ground balls
to his left at Yankee Stadium,
nor soft opposite field singles
to right at Municipal, but

instead moments with his
beautiful Vivian when time itself
seemed altered; and bedtime
story time in the nursery
with his three tow-headed children;
and the belly-pained laughter
with his lifelong quail-hunting
buddies. These moments, and his
unswerving humility,
whisper loudest at the end . . .
and the beginning.

Only That Is Was

Stand out in the half-light
when the air seems
pluckable under maples
stretching upward in summer
silence. I once did.
Like breath, a breeze
wrinkled the stillness,
moving leaves up against
one another like lovers,
the rustling like whispers,
then was gone.
I alone felt it,
heard it, missed it,
in those glimpsed
moments, not knowing
when it might return . . .
only knowing that it was,
and that I had been there.

—July 31, 2003

Stirring

No stirring disrupts the bare
tree branches reaching up
into the clear wintry darkness.
We walk the graveled downhill
path toward the lake from the bright
toasty confines of the cabin, as chat
underfoot speaks out into the night,
though we do not. At water's edge
we stride the length of a dock,
two planks at a time, ten steps,
maybe twelve, then stop; leaning
over the edge, we see more stars
than blackness above, below us
even more stars reflected
by the mirrored night-darkened water.
As if in weightless space, we float
on silence, stirred beyond words.

Ted Williams

"... baseball is counterpoint: stability vying with volatility, tradition with the quest for a new edge, ancient rhythms and ever-new blood."

—A. Bartlett Giamatti, A Great and Glorious Game, *p. 104*

The Shortstop and the Second Baseman

The shortstop drove hard
always, hard-charging,
striving, innovating, motivating,
inventing, reinventing, leave
a place better than you
found it. The second baseman
held back, quiet-voiced, afraid
to offend, do no harm, leave
a place as you found it. Yet,
the polar pair found their
separate traits created the soft steps
and hard throws of the 6-4-3
inning ending double play,
simultaneously blending
the corporate operations and
motioned poetry of baseball.

October Daughter, 2013

Adam Wainwright dueling
Jon Lester. Game Five tied
1-1. World Series tied
2-2 with hometown
St. Louis fans twirling
madly their towels
overhead, great loud
fans packed in for
the tension of a rematch,
Cardinals-Red Sox from 1967,
or 1946, or 2004 gluing us
to the TV, when Catherine
asks, "Daddy, will you help
me dress my dolls for
bed?" What's a two on,
two out, full count
to that? Let me know
if he got out of the inning.

Deep Faults

I wear a Yankees cap
when I mow the yard,
now streaked and rimmed
and splotched white
from dried sweat, faded
purple from hours and hours
of bright hot summer work,
stored in the garage in blistered
heat and crackling cold.
Never would I mistreat
my hat of the cash poor Royals
with such abuse, maybe
because deep faults in my
character brood bitter
that big money talks,
people sway, greed alters,
and at least for now,
power wins.

Sling

We live on a glass
planet, in skins of crystal,
protecting organs made
of porcelain, all as beautiful
as the sun-sparkled stream
from which are taken
seven smooth stones we like
to sling at each other.

Glimpses, 1914

They were young
and away from home
for the first time—
scared, cold, wet,
mud-caked. Witnesses
insist the first salvo
came from the Germans,
"Stille Nacht, Heilige
Nacht" shattering
the frozen evening lull.
Returning fire, "The First
Noel" launched
from the British trenches
across the wired wasteland,
both sides then exchanging
carols like musical artillery
shells. As daylight
broke, handshakes
and gifts replaced
song . . . and shouts
of soccer shuttled
combat to the rear,
as officers scratched
their whiskerless

. .

all this just a glimpse
through the mist, toward
coming in out of the wind,
the great entropy
over.

—February 22, 2013

Alcatraz Rules

Out on the windswept,
white-capped bay, on
a dusty small diamond
surrounded by gray
walls, only slap hitters
are valued, and pitchers
who keep the ball
down in the zone, for
anything hit over
the wall is an out,
the ball gone, irretrievable,
the ball game over,
a sad return to time,
according to Alcatraz rules.

Beginnings

Few in this age tolerate
surrender, bringing
to mind unacceptable
weakness, failure,
loss, appeasement, yet
anyone belonging
to baseball knows
surrender is the crucial
element—to abilities, to
coaching, to teammates, to
nerves to realize potential. Rather
than an ending, surrender
sweeps in beginnings when
dreams become World Series
game-tying sprints from third.

The Coldest Days

I remember well the long-
ago melted summer
day they told us
of his drowning. And
I recall that except
on the coldest days
he wore shorts, the old
bright Dodger brand
of our youth, the kind
that left angled tan lines
on our skinny legs, after
days and days of sunlit
neighborhood backyard
baseball, our games
played slanted, a tough
run uphill to first base
after a hit. Then
there was the wool gray day
his brother sat alone
in our rope swing, surveying
snow-frosted black limbs
of a walnut tree—our summertime
foul pole—having dragged two
runner sleds down

our backyard hill—a hill
that seemed much steeper
on this coldest of days.

Dusk, 1938

As darkness fell on Wrigley
that late September twilight,
Gabby Hartnett crushed
a Pittsburgh fastball over
the newly planted ivy,
on the way to a Cubbies pennant,
just seconds before the game
was to be called due
to darkness. An ocean
away, European leaders
confronted each other
as well on this day, Neville
Chamberlain throwing
the best he had, Hitler
crushing the pitch,
as darkness fell on Wrigley,
and everywhere else.

Firestorm Earth

Curiously silent lightning sears
the darkened sky far off away
to the east like cloud-borne
armies locked in distant combat.
From this vantage point,
the massive flashing poses
no threat, and silhouetted
giant thunderheads
rivet in place all who watch;
yet soon, thoughts drift
toward those near the raging
tumult, wondering if they
peer through lightless
windows at the storm,
much as stars above firestorm
earth seem to peek through
easterly racing wisps of clouds.

—*August 18, 2002*

Little gods

We have been accused
in our past, of worshipping
baseball, expanding our
moments with its foul
lines extending into eternity,
its clocklessness, its simple
complexity, its goal of home,
its slow summer daydreams.

We have been accused, later,
of worshipping football
with its military regimented
clock-controlled violence
we can watch from warm
armchairs on cold autumn afternoons.

We have been accused
of worshipping sex, at
its best a mutual self-
surrender, a simultaneous
giving and receiving, a
mysterious Holy ground,
communion outside of time.

Now we worship small
screens we lower our eyes
to by the minute as if in prayer
to little gods, addicted,
disconnecting us in ways
we should not be disconnected,
connecting us in ways
we should not be connected,
leading us down the promised
newest, fastest, moment-stealing,
wide, distracted way.

Such Signs

Sycamores with skirts of cedars
stand sentinel over Turkey Creek,
wintering alfalfa fields nearly
bronze under overcast skies. Under
layers of years, deep in our past,
these trees, their bleached trunks
and branches distinctly white
from miles away, foretold water,
life itself, flowing through wooded
valleys. Such signs are lost
to a people who do not even
look up long enough to notice.

—December 29, 2008
in Jefferson City, MO

"There comes a time when every summer will have something of autumn about it."

—*A. Bartlett Giamatti,* A Great and Glorious Game, *p. 8*

This Time Last Year

For Marilyn

We watch your mother
waste away, dying
so slowly, so quickly,
the future and the past
converging at her
bedside, then exploding
apart into splinters. How
can we ever again
admire humanity's flailing,
knowing what we now
know? How can we
put faith in the dust
of the physical, the material?
She shrinks before our eyes.
We know she is there,
somewhere, yet she seems
strangely alien, which
in itself is its own pain.
I watch your face
tonight, the face
I have loved so long,
so deeply, contort beyond
tears, as I find no words.

There are no words.
Outside, the November
darkness weighs much more
than this time last year.

—November 6, 2014

Last Minutes

To Marilyn, In Memory of Marlis Meyer

I will not remember her
as she was in that hospital
bed in her last minutes, a
windy sunny Monday, though
I am thankful we were there. Instead,
I will remember standing elbow
to elbow with her at the stove top
flipping pancakes on bright spring
break Sunday mornings; and
the sweetness of her cinder cake;
and her grandkid trips to Downtown
Book and Toy; and the sweltering
family 4th's, three houses past
the city limits—firecrackers!; and
the way she carefully cut Kansas
City Royals articles out of the News-
Tribune to send to her son-in-law,
even though she was a Cardinals
fan. She glued her family together.

You entered life through her door.
For those and countless more,
I will remember her.

—November 10, 2014
Holts Summit, Missouri

I. The Beaning of Ray Chapman

August 16, 1920

I wonder what Ray Chapman
ate for breakfast that August
New York morning, long
ago. Were his taste buds
heightened with realization
of time closing in, the white
mouse and the black mouse
gnawing away the branch
he was sitting on? Or did
the bacon taste as always?
When was the last time
he was with Katie? Had it
pleased her? Did he think
of her often, her belly
beginning to swell
with passing life? Did he ponder
meaning or meaninglessness
of the universe? Or maybe
this was a day just like
any other, when the high
rising fastball cracked open
that moment in the fifth inning

and all voices became dim,
small, until there was only
one, the final answer
enveloping Ray Chapman,
as it will us all.

II. The Beaning of Katie Chapman

April 21, 1928

News of the rising Mays fastball
that day at the Polo Grounds found
its way by phone to Cleveland, to
Katie, her frantic trip to New York
too late to tell her Ray goodbye—
six months later birthing their
daughter. Even later, trying on
courage like a mask, she remarried, yet
never could shake the dancing
laugh, the laughing songs, the
grinning tousle-haired Ray, the
soul hole too deep, the darkness
too thick, giving up, leaning in
to her own high rising fastball.

III. Plans

August 15, 1920

Ray agreed to quit the game,
for Katie, at the end of the season,
to work for her rich Daddy,
in Cleveland, to live a sun-dappled
life of wealth, to raise a son . . .
or daughter?! who knew?
Katie counts the days
until her laughing Ray
lets go the bone-jarring, harsh,
violent orb of baseball. Soon
it will be done. They have plans.

IV. The Beaning of Rae Chapman

April 21, 1929

Eight years ago,
for obvious reasons,
Katie named her Rae.
Now orphaned, Rae lays ill
and dying, as Ellington's
jazz stomps, as flappers
flap, as Satchmo
asks if Gabriel likes
his music, the roaring
not yet knocked out
of the 1920s, very few
guessing the massive
Crash fast approaching,
maybe caused by one
world war, surely causing
the next bigger one . . . so
much suffering to come . . .
as she, so young, the last
Chapman to cross over,
runs laughing into the Mystery
that will envelop us all,
safe at home.

The Old Brewery

A mile or so west of Boonville,
up-river from Harley Park, and
very near the roiling of the Missouri
sliding with force and grace
toward the Mississippi and the sea,
the remains of stone-masoned
walls and arches rise within
the shadow of deep woods
and undergrowth like jungled
ruins of ancient Mayans. On
railroad tracks glinting in
the summer heat, an old man
stands, his back to the river,
looking uphill at the crumbling
before him, untiring nature's
reclamation. The man remembers
this place during his childhood,
deserted then yet still intact
and open, hillside and buildings
naked to the gilded river and sun
and sky, walls towering above
him. Below he knows was once
a landing, steamboats loading
and unloading, when great rivers
were thoroughfares, long ago.
Throughout his life, he has ventured

here, with his parents; with his wife;
with his daughters; with his grandsons;
and now, alone. Today, somehow
knowing this is the end of such hikes,
the dignity of this place allows him
the contemplation of graceful sliding
into the mysterious.

Shadows Across Kansas

These green island towns,
surrounded not by water
but by wheat, drift by only
slightly faster than air
schooners of white cumulus
casting shadows across Kansas,
clouds always looking
to me like softly lined Texas
League singles over shortstop,
seen from the upper deck.

Surrender

You cannot play this game
aiming and tight, intent
on white knuckle, self-consuming
control. After all the effort,
training, preparation, sacrifice,
there must be an air of surrender,
a letting-go of self and time,
if you want to make the crooked
ways straight, find yourself
new, and not grow weary.

Willie Mays

"I want to go down on the field and play with the boys."

—Loren Michael Broaddus, age 4, at Hammons Field, Springfield, Missouri

"As a boy, I always wanted to be a Major League baseball pitcher."

—Andy Bryan, pastor, Campbell United Methodist Church

Walnut, 1975

Really, it was a quarter
of a walnut center,
dried and sharp, that
the boy slid over
playing backyard baseball,
ripping a gash in his knee
his brother thought
above the kneecap,
his mother below.
Stitched up, immobile,
leg elevated, the boy
suffered clear October air
to quit beckoning . . . until,
due to his injury, he got
to stay up late
on a school night to see
Game Six of the World Series,
Red Sox-Reds,
Fisk forcing a Game Seven,
homering in the twelfth
off the Green Monster
foul pole, waving, willing
it fair, rounding the bases
exuberant as a little boy.

Forbidden

For Zach Davis

The kid in the third
row looks at me
straight-faced and says,
"Funny isn't funny
unless funny is forbidden."
I write it down to use
in a poem someday,
but most likely
never will.

The Ball Bag

Made of heavy canvas,
it was large enough
for a boy to crawl
into, if it wasn't full,
which it was—
of baseballs, bats,
catcher's equipment,
and an old unclaimed
glove from last season—
an aroma present
strangely mixed of leather,
wood, mildew, magic, on
a not quite warm
overcast spring day,
its contents dumped
onto greening grass,
this first day of practice,
infielders separating
from outfielders, boys
anticipating nothing
except this present
boyhood moment.

Soaked

Back then, we are boys
still, heading out school
doors for morning recess
carrying bats, ball, gloves,
bases—the grass dew-sparkled
on the long walk to the cool
shadows of trees stretching
across our grassy diamond.
One boy is nicknamed Garvey;
another Patek; a third
Joe Charboneau, who we heard
could open bottle caps with
his eye socket. Much later,
one of us will die young;
one battles alcoholism;
a third becomes a senator,
yet on this clear spring
morning little matters
except soft singles over second,
skinny legs running wildly
around first, the dew soaking
our blue jeans to the knees.

Charlie's Rainbow

Obnoxiously, Charlie shouts out
to anyone and no one, "Hey,
can you give me a ride
to Forsyth to pick up
my truck? I've got to check
on my cattle!" each syllable
tipping anger. The regulars
quit hearing long ago. It
is the visitor who weighs
words and place on mental
scales, wondering if indeed
truck and cattle are fact
or delusion, waiting three
hours away in Forsyth.

Independence Day they all
meet in the dining hall
of the Alzheimer's unit
and after ice cream with
red, blue, and white sprinkles
Charlie stands up, eyes
sparkling, and in a clear,

beautiful Irish tenor
sings Dorothy's classic,
ending with
"Why, oh why can't I?"
the words lingering in the air
like the remembered laughter
of a child now long grown.

Radio

For my Mom

She carried around
a radio, tuned in to baseball,
no room in the house out of earshot
of the Royals of my youth,
the voices of Denny Matthews
and Fred White the backsplash
of 1970s childhood summers.

Dusty and Nicky

For my Dad, and his Dad

Two boys play catch
on a green-gold and dappled
afternoon as global war rages
far away, swastikas and rising
suns never too far out
of mind. "Pop" into Dusty's
mitt . . . "Pop" into Nicky's
mitt. Back and forth,
both imagination
and distraction coating
each throw and catch,
until one gets away,
breaking a shingle
on the neighbor's barn,
the two boys snapped
back into time and space,
scared, wondering what to do,
looking around for witnesses
in this age of corporal
punishment, the game
of catch abruptly ending.
After silence becomes
the solution, Dusty's
father asks quietly

at supper that night,
what are you planning
to do about that shingle?
Dusty now knowing
his father knew all along,
a lesson about secrets,
and fathers, not soon forgotten.

Local Boys

Teams of the South Baldwin League
played twice a week, April to September,
with names like Magnolia Springs, Fairhope,
Summerdale, Foley, Silver Hill, and
Bon Secour. On Sundays, all ages watched
heated rivalries and players they admired
more than DiMaggio or Williams or even
Musial. Lower Alabama humidity and heat
soaked both players and fans, salty breezes
off the Gulf offering the only relief,
the outcomes of games resting on local boys,
boys soon headed for the meat grinder of
Cold War Korea. These ball fields, presently
long overgrown, are forgotten,
as tourists drive past on Highway 59,
past the outlet mall and the real estate offices
toward the best corporate-owned, high-rise
lined beaches in North America.

"I'd rather be the shortest player in the Major Leagues than the tallest player in the Minors."

—Fred Patek

"You don't have to weigh two-hundred and fifty pounds to make good in baseball and you don't have to be six-foot-seven either. I like that."

—Harry S. Truman

Joe DiMaggio

Twenty Years Since

We held hands,
though the dog's
leash wrapped
around our wrists
held our holding, as
we walked into
the slanted October
morning, crisp
against our skin,
light shimmering
through brilliant
dying leaves,
twenty years since
my porch swing
proposal, your
touch moving me
still in the stillness.

—*October 11, 2016*

Fred Patek, Meet Mr. McBeevee

A 5'4" shortstop becomes
a seventies two-time All-Star.
No one dreams that up, or
predicts it, or believes it
ahead of time. Impossible.
Sometimes the illogical
spins itself inside out
when reality speaks so softly
of the cannon arm, the water
bug quickness, the triple hitting
speed, the immeasurable heart.

It also turns out that, after all
the adult smug smiles turn
to arrogant, alarmed, even angry
disbelief, as red-headed
Opie continues to refuse
logic, Mr. McBeevee actually
does exist, with twelve extra
hands, the walking in treetops,
the shiny hat,
blowing smoke out
his ear, and all that impossible
jingling—seeming to signal
to take great care
what you disbelieve.

Will

If one could will oneself
short, the boy did when
he was ten, all because
of Fred Patek, the shortest
player in the Majors, his
hero. And the boy was.
Short.

"I always listen to ballgames, or jazz, on my front porch swing," says the fan. "My house is an old, 1930s fieldstone bungalow."

"You know, that's how I always picture people listening," replies Ryan Lefebvre, Royals radio broadcaster at a winter caravan, 2003

Folding Moments

The high white sky
betrays the midday
summer heat, humidity
almost able to be leaned
into, velvety against
the skin. A cobalt blue
car rolls slowly past
bright orange tiger lilies
shouting out silently
into overcast air
to no one in particular,
yet also seeming
to listen intently
to jazz from across
the vast expanse
of Phelps Grove Park,
Grant Green's sextet
effortlessly folding
one idle moment into the next.

Rattletraps, 2015

I remember thinking,
and maybe even saying,
during the hundred-loss
seasons of '04, '05, '06,
how difficult it would be
if the Royals contended
again, or even won it
all. No more comfort
of predictable misery,
almost feeling even then
the rattletraps beginning,
the involuntary shakes,
watching the entire
postseason standing up,
too nervous to sit still,
the boys fearless, fast,
relentless, coming
from behind over
and over, keeping
the line moving,
befuddling the numbers,
the poetry of small ball
alive in an unpoetic age.

"Why is home plate not called fourth base?"

—*A. Bartlett Giamatti,* A Great and Glorious Game

Nearing Home

For Bill Virdon

On a bright noon Saturday
out on a sun-soaked Little
League baseball field, each
team of boys in bright colored
uniforms line each base path,
shoulder to shoulder, after being
announced on this Opening
Day in May. A man with a cane
shuffles slowly toward home
plate, the honored guest, his name
now attached to the field—
a rookie of the year, a gold
glove center fielder, a
World Series Champion,
a Major League manager,
baseball in his veins,
still handsome in his Pirates cap—
now frail and gray, surrounded
by eager ten-year-olds who
cannot recognize greatness,
and who can hardly imagine
an old man young, an old man
slowly nearing home.

Harley Park, Boonville

There was something
about the light that evening,
surrounded by deep darkness,
seen from an overlooking
hill, as we came across
the brightly lit ballpark, a game
in progress, the pitcher
letting loose his pitch,
each fielder rising
to his toes, evident even
from this distance—light
like the glow of a fire
after a rain-soaked walk;
a song not heard
since childhood; a nostalgia
for something never known;
the familiar aroma
of one deeply loved; or
hometown roots returned to.

Passing Through

It's been thirty years since
he played his last baseball
game, breathing his last
breath as a shortstop, deeply
feeling something inside
turn, a passing through,
into a life unimagined.

Walnut Street Inn

Rich August evening
sunlight streams through
the west window
of the Findley room,
surrounded by a deep
high-ceilinged past
painted golden, every
inch of you illuminated
in the glow, the light
like it must have been
for other long-ago lovers
long gone, the past,
the future, the present,
converging into one.

Home

Out on the base paths,
in bright air and sharp
shadow of high adventure,
there is daring and danger,
quicksilver decision making,
signals to decipher,
all calling for intelligence,
intuition, speed, risking
triumph, disaster, pain, glory,
losing consciousness of life
itself, the moment so focused
on running well, running smart,
savoring . . . yet
always mindful of,
always striving for,
home.

"The boomer is motivated by greed, the desire for money, property, and therefore power . . . Stickers on the contrary are motivated by affection, by such love for a place and its life that they want to preserve it and remain in it."

—*Wendell Berry,* It All Turns on Affection, *p. 11*

At the Intersection Schulz and Berry

Standing very alone
on that impossibly
humped pitcher's
mound, longing
in winter, hopeful
in spring, realistic
before autumn, Charlie
Brown is a loser among
winners, a sticker among
boomers, a quiet
soul surrounded by
loudness, dogged
in a fickle, faithless world.

"I never feel more at home than at a ballgame."

—*Robert Frost*

This photograph was taken somewhere around the year 1946, in Boonville, Missouri. The adult pictured is Carrie. The older girl is my mother, Nancy, with her cousin, Christi. This photo has dug itself deep inside me, capturing, I'm afraid, all the complexities of race in America.

Carrie loved Joe DiMaggio, and later Mickey Mantle, during the Jackie Robinson era. I have always loved those underdog Dodger teams, and I've always wondered why Carrie chose to live and die with the Yankees. No one in my family really knows, except that the Yankees won.

A tower of strength and pride and stability and intelligence, with a mind of her own, Carrie lived in an age rigged against her. Her options were severely limited due to institutional racism, yet her influence on my mother was immense. She loved and was loved. She also passed down, through my mother, the amazing game of baseball, whether or not she chose Jackie or Joe . . .

Acknowledgments

I would like to thank my friend Jo Van Arkel, and her assistant Aarin Song, of Pencil Box Press, where this work appeared in an earlier form. In the autumn of my junior year in college, I took a creative writing class on a whim. The professor was Jo Van Arkel. The world never again looked the same. Thank you, Jo.

I would also like to thank editors William McGill of *Spitball: A Literary Baseball Magazine*, and Hayley Fraser of THINK Magazine, where a number of these pieces have previously been published.

Lastly, I would like to thank Patty Rice, for her kindness and diligence, and Andrews McMeel Publishing. Thank you for taking these poems places I never thought they would go. I will always be grateful.

Thank you Marilyn, for still taking my breath away when you walk into a room.

About the Author

Loren Broaddus lives in Springfield, Missouri, with his wife Marilyn, their two children, and their dog Barney. They inspire him every day. He teaches history at Kickapoo High School. Previously, he has written two limited edition chapbooks, *Weight* and *The Birthing Tree*.

Index

Andrews McMeel Publishing
a division of Andrews McMeel Universal
1130 Walnut Street, Kansas City, Missouri 64106

www.andrewsmcmeel.com

19 20 21 22 23 BVG 10 9 8 7 6 5 4 3 2 1

ISBN: 978-1-5248-5249-8

Library of Congress Control Number: 2019939409

Editor: Patty Rice
Art Director: Holly Swayne
Production Editor: Margaret Daniels
Production Manager: Cliff Koehler
Cover and interior illustrations: Aarin Song